CONTENTMENT

CONTENTMENT

Warren W. Wiersbe

VICTOR BOOKS

A DIVISION OF SCRIPTURE PRESS PUBLICATIONS INC.
USA CANADA ENGLAND

Copyediting: Afton Rorvik
Cover Design: Grace K. Chan Mallette

Library of Congress Cataloging-in-Publication Data

Wiersbe, Warren W.
    Contentment / Warren W. Wiersbe.
        p.   cm.
        1. Bible O.T.   Ecclesiastes—Devotional literature.
    2. Devotional calendars. I. Title.
    BS1475.4.W55   1994
    242'.2—dc20

                                                                94-7622
                                                                CIP

© 1994 by SP Publications, Inc. All rights reserved. Printed in the United States of America.

1 2 3 4 5 6 7 8 9 10 Printing/Year 98 97 96 95 94

If you are studying *Be Satisfied* in a Sunday School class or small group, this 30-Day Devotional will complement your study. Each devotional is adapted from a chapter in *Be Satisfied*. The following chart indicates the correlation. You may, of course, use this book without reference to *Be Satisfied*.

Be Satisfied **Contentment**

Book Chapter	30-Day Devotional
1	Days 1, 2, and 3
2	Days 4, 5, and 6
3	Days 7, 8, and 9
4	Days 10 and 11
5	Days 12 and 13
6	Days 14 and 15
7	Days 16, 17, and 18
8	Days 19, 20, and 21
9	Days 22 and 23
10	Days 24, 25, and 26
11	Days 27 and 28
12	Days 29 and 30

INTRODUCTION

"People are never free of trying to be content."

Ecologist Murray Brookchin wrote that in the June 1, 1992 issue of the London *Independent;* and more than a century earlier, the American naturalist Henry David Thoreau wrote, "The mass of men lead lives of quiet desperation."

Both men are right.

Today, we can go to the drugstore and buy mood elevators and even buy sleep, but we can't buy peace and contentment. If we want to escape the "rat race," we can visit a theme park and purchase hours of entertainment; but the "rat race" will still be there when we walk out the gate.

True contentment is a matter of *the inner person:* having the right priorities, measuring life by the right standards, focusing on the right goals, and exercising the right faith. It means taking God into every area of your life and letting Him have control.

If anybody knew the folly of living for the "rat race" (he called it "chasing after the wind"), it was King Solomon. He *had* everything and he *tried* everything, and he recorded his experiments and experiences for us to read in an ancient book we call Ecclesiastes – "The Preacher."

The most recent self-help manual in the bookstore doesn't begin to give you the insights that Solomon shares in this journal of a man who "tried to catch the wind." Solomon writes about success, leadership, life goals, social injustice, sex and marriage, money, and even old age and death. He honestly records his own feelings and failures and the lessons he learned from these experiments in the laboratory of life. He paid the price — you get all the benefits of his wisdom!

He tells you the master secret of having contentment in a world that wants to rob you of peace. Solomon points the way to the kind of "lifestyle" that makes living worthwhile and saves you from the dead-end streets of modern civilization.

Jesus said, "I have come that they may have life, and have it to the full" (John 10:10).

Solomon knew about that abundant life centuries ago, and you can know about it today. As each day you learn from King Solomon, you'll discover that life can be satisfying and successful when you walk with God and trust Him.

— Warren W. Wiersbe

*My thanks to Stan Campbell,
who compiled the contents of this book
and added thought-provoking questions
to enrich your personal growth.*

Read **Ecclesiastes 1:1**

Solomon's Sequel

Nowhere in this book did the author give his name, but the descriptions he gave of himself and his experiences would indicate that the writer was King Solomon. Solomon began his reign as a humble servant of the Lord, seeking God's wisdom and help (1 Kings 3:5-15). As he grew older, his heart turned away from Jehovah to the false gods of the many wives he had taken from foreign lands (1 Kings 11:1ff). These marriages were motivated primarily by politics, not love, as Solomon sought alliances with the nations around Israel.

No amount of money or authority could stop the silent but sure ripening of divine judgment. The famous Scottish preacher Alexander Whyte said that "the secret worm . . . was gnawing all the time in the royal staff upon which Solomon leaned." The king's latter years were miserable because God removed His hand of blessing (1 Kings 11) and maintained Solomon's throne only because of His promise to David.

Ecclesiastes appears to be the kind of book a person would write near the close of life, reflecting on

> *"The words of the Teacher, son of David,*
> *king in Jerusalem"*
> *(Ecclesiastes 1:1).*

....

life's experiences and the lessons learned. Solomon probably wrote Proverbs and the Song of Solomon during the years he faithfully walked with God; and near the end of his life, he wrote Ecclesiastes. There is no record that King Solomon repented and turned to the Lord, but his message in Ecclesiastes suggests that he did.

Applying God's Truth:

1. What is the most foolish thing you've done out of love for someone?

2. If the wisest man who ever lived could not remain faithful to God, do you think it's realistic to expect that you can? Explain.

3. Based on Solomon's experiences, what would you say might be more important than wisdom in regard to continual spiritual growth?

.... **11**

Read **Ecclesiastes 1:2**

Whether Vain

....

"Vanity of vanities," lamented Solomon, "all is vanity!" (according to the *King James Version* of v. 2). Solomon liked that word "vanity"; he used it thirty-eight times in Ecclesiastes as he wrote about life "under the sun." The word means "emptiness, futility, vapor, that which vanishes quickly and leaves nothing behind."

From the human point of view ("under the sun"), life does appear futile, and it is easy for us to get pessimistic. The Jewish writer Sholom Aleichem once described life as "a blister on top of a tumor, and a boil on top of that." You can almost feel that definition!

The American poet Carl Sandburg compared life to "an onion — you peel it off one layer at a time, and sometimes you weep." And British playwright George Bernard Shaw said that life was "a series of inspired follies."

What a relief to turn from these pessimistic views and hear Jesus Christ say, "I have come that they may have life, and have it to the full" (John 10:10). Or to read Paul's majestic declaration, "Therefore, my dear

> " 'Meaningless! Meaningless!' says the
> Teacher. 'Utterly meaningless!
> Everything is meaningless' "
> *(Ecclesiastes 1:2).*

....

brothers, stand firm. Let nothing move you. Always
give yourselves fully to the work of the Lord, because
you know that your labor in the Lord is not in vain"
(1 Cor. 15:58).

Life is "not in vain" if it is lived according to the will
of God, and that is what Solomon teaches in this
neglected and often misunderstood book.

Applying God's Truth:

1. Have you ever gone through periods when you
    considered your life and felt all was vanity
    (meaningless)?

2. How would you define your current philosophy of
    life in a couple of sentences?

3. What relationships and activities provide the most
    meaning in your life?

Read **Ecclesiastes 1:3**

Problems Then and Now

....

What is the practical application of this book for us today? Is Ecclesiastes nothing but an interesting exhibit in a religious museum, or does it have a message for people in the Space Age?

Its message is for today. After all, the society which Solomon investigated a millennium before the birth of Christ was not too different from our world today. Solomon saw injustice to the poor, crooked politics, incompetent leaders, guilty people allowed to commit more crime, materialism, and a desire for "the good old days." It sounds up-to-date, doesn't it?

If you have never trusted Jesus Christ as your Savior, then this book urges you to do so without delay. Why? Because no matter how much wealth, education, or social prestige you may have, life without God is futile. You are only "chasing after the wind" if you expect to find satisfaction and personal fulfillment in the things of the world. "What good is it for a man to gain the whole world, yet forfeit his soul?" asked Jesus (Mark 8:36).

Solomon experimented with life and discovered

"What does man gain from all his labor at
which he toils under the sun?"
(Ecclesiastes 1:3)

....

that there was no lasting satisfaction in possessions,
pleasures, power, or prestige. He had everything, yet
his life was empty! There is no need for you and me to
repeat these experiments. Let's accept Solomon's
conclusions and avoid the heartache and pain that
must be endured when you experiment in the
laboratory of life.

Applying God's Truth:

1. What have you witnessed lately that caused you to
   question the fairness of life?

2. What are some of the things you've tried in an
   attempt to bring more meaning to life?

3. How would you contrast the quality of your life
   before a relationship with Jesus with life
   afterward?

Read **Ecclesiastes 1:4-8**

As Sure as the World

....

From the human point of view, nothing seems more permanent and durable than the planet on which we live. When we say that something is "as sure as the world," we are echoing Solomon's confidence in the permanence of planet Earth. With all of its diversity, nature is uniform enough in its operation that we can discover its "laws" and put them to work for us. In fact, it is this "dependability" that is the basis for modern science.

Nature is permanent, but man is transient, a mere pilgrim on earth. His pilgrimage is a brief one, for death finally claims him. At the very beginning of his book, Solomon introduced a topic frequently mentioned in Ecclesiastes: the brevity of life and the certainty of death.

Individuals and families come and go, nations and empires rise and fall, but nothing changes, for the world remains the same. Thomas Carlyle called history "a mighty drama, enacted upon the theater of time, with suns for lamps and eternity for a background." Solomon would add that the costumes and sets may occasionally change, but the actors and

> *"Generations come and generations go, but
> the earth remains forever"*
> *(Ecclesiastes 1:4).*

....

the script remain pretty much the same; and that's as
sure as the world.

Applying God's Truth:

1. How frequently do you think about your inevitable
   death? How does it make you feel?

2. How do you try to ensure that you're making the
   most of your life while you have the opportunity?

3. As a member of your generation, how well are you
   connected to the older generation(s) as well as the
   younger one(s)?

Read **Ecclesiastes 1:9-11**

Everything Old Is New Again

A young man approached me at a conference and asked if he could share some new ideas for youth ministry. He was very enthusiastic as he outlined his program; but the longer I listened, the more familiar his ideas became. I encouraged him to put his ideas into practice, but then told him that we had done all of those things in Youth for Christ before he was born, and that YFC workers were still doing them. He was a bit stunned to discover that there was indeed nothing new under the sun.

Solomon wrote, of course, about the basic principles of life and not about methods. As the familiar couplet puts it: Methods are many, principles are few/methods always change, principles never do. The ancient thinkers knew this. The Stoic philosopher Marcus Aurelius wrote, "They that come after us will see nothing new, and they who went before us saw nothing more than we have seen." The only people who really think they have seen something new are those whose experience is limited or whose vision can't penetrate beneath the surface of things. Because something is recent, they think it is new; they mistake novelty for originality.

*"Is there anything of which one can say,
'Look! This is something new'? It was
here already, long ago; it was here before
our time"*
(Ecclesiastes 1:10).

....

Applying God's Truth:

1. What are some of the principles you've held
   throughout your life that are identical to those of
   your parents and preceding generations?

2. How would you distinguish between *novelty* and
   originality?

3. If it's true that there is no new thing under the sun,
   why do you think people today put so much
   emphasis on "new and improved," "new and
   better," and other promises of hitherto
   undiscovered products and services?

DAY 6

Read **Ecclesiastes 1:12-18**

Living in Circles
....

When Adam and Eve sinned, they did get an experiential knowledge of good and evil; but, since they were alienated from God, this knowledge only added to their sorrows. It has been that way with man ever since. Whether it be jet planes, insecticides, or television, each advance in human knowledge and achievement only creates a new set of problems for society.

For some people, life may be monotonous and meaningless; but it doesn't have to be. For the Christian believer, life is an open door, not a closed circle; there are daily experiences of new blessings from the Lord. True, we can't explain everything; but life is not built on explanations: it's built on promises — and we have plenty of promises in God's Word!

The scientist tells us that the world is a closed system and nothing is changed. The historian tells us that life is a closed book and nothing is new. The philosopher tells us that life is a deep problem and nothing is understood.

But Jesus Christ is "the power of God and the wisdom of God" (1 Cor. 1:24), and He has

> *"I applied myself to the understanding of wisdom, and also of madness and folly, but I learned that this, too, is a chasing after the wind. For with much wisdom comes much sorrow; the more knowledge, the more grief"*
> *(Ecclesiastes 1:17-18).*

....

miraculously broken into history to bring new life to all who trust Him. If you are "living in circles," then turn your life over to Him.

Applying God's Truth:

1. Do you think Solomon's observation that "in much wisdom is much grief" is the same as declaring that "ignorance is bliss"? Why?

2. Do you agree that in much wisdom is much grief? Give some specific examples to support your answer.

3. In what ways do you feel you may be "living in circles"?

Read **Ecclesiastes 2:1-11**

When Pleasure Is Treasured

....

Today's world is pleasure-mad. Millions of people will pay almost any amount of money to "buy experiences" and temporarily escape the burdens of life. While there is nothing wrong with innocent fun, the person who builds his or her life only on seeking pleasure is bound to be disappointed in the end.

Why? For one thing, pleasure-seeking usually becomes a selfish endeavor; and selfishness destroys true joy. People who live for pleasure often exploit others to get what they want, and they end up with broken relationships as well as empty hearts. *People are more important than things and thrills.* We are to be channels, not reservoirs; the greatest joy comes when we share God's pleasures with others.

If you live for pleasure alone, enjoyment will decrease unless the intensity of the pleasure increases. Then you reach a point of diminishing returns when there is little or no enjoyment at all, only bondage. For example, the more that people drink, the less enjoyment they get out of it. This means they must have more drinks and stronger drinks in order to have pleasure; the sad result is desire without satisfaction.

"I denied myself nothing my eyes desired; I refused my heart no pleasure. . . . Yet when I surveyed all that my hands had done . . . everything was meaningless"
(Ecclesiastes 2:10-11).

....

Instead of alcohol, substitute drugs, gambling, sex, money, fame, or any other pursuit, and the principle will hold true: when pleasure alone is the center of life, the result will ultimately be disappointment and emptiness.

Applying God's Truth:

1. On a scale of 1 (least) to 10 (most), to what extent would you say you are a pleasure-seeker?

2. In what ways do people you know try to use pleasure to find fulfillment in life?

3. How can you enjoy life to the fullest, without having your pleasurable experiences diminish in effectiveness?

DAY 8

Read **Ecclesiastes 2:12-23**

Money Management

．．．．．．．．．．．．．．．．．．．．．．．．．．．．．．．．．．．．．

Solomon was born wealthy, and great wealth came to him because he was the king. But he was looking at life "under the sun" and speaking for the "common people" who were listening to his discussion. The day would come when Solomon would die and leave everything to his successor. This reminds us of our Lord's warning in the Parable of the Rich Fool (Luke 12:13-21) and Paul's words in 1 Timothy 6:7-10. A Jewish proverb says, "There are no pockets in shrouds."

Money is a medium of exchange. Unless it is spent, it can do little or nothing for you. You can't eat money, but you can use it to buy food. It will not keep you warm, but it will purchase fuel. A writer in *The Wall Street Journal* called money "an article which may be used as a universal passport to everywhere except heaven, and as a universal provider of everything except happiness."

Of course, you and I are *stewards* of our wealth; God is the Provider (Deut. 8:18) and the Owner, and we have the privilege of enjoying it and using it for His glory. One day we will have to give an account of what

24 ．．．．．．．．．．．．．．．．．．．．．．．．．．．．．．．．．．．

> *"I hated all the things I had toiled for under the sun, because I must leave them to the one who comes after me. And who knows whether he will be a wise man or a fool?"*
>
> *(Ecclesiastes 2:18-19)*

....

we have done with His generous gifts. While we cannot take wealth with us when we die, we can "send it ahead" as we use it today according to God's will (Matt. 6:19-34).

Applying God's Truth:

1. To what extent would you say you are concerned about leaving a good inheritance for your children? Do you wonder if they will appreciate it as they should?

2. What is your philosophy of money? How much importance do you think it deserves?

3. What does it mean to you to be a "steward" of your wealth?

Read **Ecclesiastes 2:24-26**

Eat, Drink, and Be Thankful

....

Solomon is not advocating "Eat, drink, and be merry, for tomorrow we die!" That is the philosophy of fatalism, not faith. Rather, he is saying, "Thank God for what you do have, and enjoy it to the glory of God." Paul gave his approval to this attitude when he exhorted us to trust "in God, who richly provides us with everything for our enjoyment" (1 Tim. 6:17).

Solomon made it clear that not only were the blessings from God, but even the enjoyment of the blessings was God's gift to us (v. 24). He considered it "evil" if a person had all the blessings of life from God but could not enjoy them (6:1-5). It is easy to see why the Jewish people read Ecclesiastes at the Feast of Tabernacles, for Tabernacles is their great time of thanksgiving and rejoicing for God's abundant provision of their needs. The farmer who prayed at the table, "Thanks for food and for good digestion" knew what Solomon was writing about.

The important thing is that we seek to please the Lord (v. 26) and trust Him to meet every need. God wants to give us wisdom, knowledge, and joy; these three gifts enable us to appreciate God's blessings and

> *"A man can do nothing better than to eat*
> *and drink and find satisfaction in his work.*
> *This too, I see, is from the hand of God, for*
> *without Him, who can eat or find*
> *enjoyment?"*
> (Ecclesiastes 2:24)

....

take pleasure in them. *It is not enough to possess*
"things"; we must also possess the kind of character
that enables us to use "things" wisely and enjoy
them properly.

Applying God's Truth:

1. What are your "Top Ten" blessings from God?

2. For each of the things you've listed, are you
   experiencing the degree of enjoyment that you feel
   you should? If not, how can you enjoy them even
   more?

3. How can you develop "the kind of character that
   enables you to use things wisely and enjoy them
   properly"?

Read **Ecclesiastes 3:1-8**

Times and Seasons

....

You don't have to be a philosopher or a scientist to know that "times and seasons'" are a regular part of life, no matter where you live. Were it not for the dependability of God-ordained "natural laws," both science and daily life would be chaotic, if not impossible. Not only are there times and seasons in this world, but there is also an overruling providence in our lives. From before our birth to the moment of our death, God is accomplishing His divine purposes, even though we may not always understand what He is doing.

Solomon affirmed that God is at work in our individual lives, seeking to accomplish His will. All of these events come from God and they are good *in their time.* The inference is plain: if we cooperate with God's timing, life will not be meaningless. Everything will be "beautiful in its time" (v. 11), even the most difficult experiences of life.

Things like abortion, birth control, mercy killing, and surrogate parenthood make it look as though man is in control of birth and death, but Solomon said otherwise. Birth and death are not human accidents;

> *"There is a time for everything, and a
> season for every activity under heaven: a
> time to be born and a time to die"*
> *(Ecclesiastes 3:1-2).*

....

they are divine appointments, for God is in control.
Psalm 139:13-16 states that God so wove us in the
womb that our genetic structure is perfect for the work
He has prepared for us to do (Eph. 2:10). We may
foolishly hasten our death, but we cannot prevent it
when our time comes, unless God so wills it.

Applying God's Truth:

1. Read Ecclesiastes 3:1-8 and identify any of the
   times and seasons you seem to be going through
   right now.

2. Can you think of an instance when recognizing
   God's timing brought meaning to your life? In what
   way?

3. How might you discover more meaning in life by
   letting go of certain things and turning to God
   instead?

Read **Ecclesiastes 3:9-22**

Enjoyment and Eternity
....

When the well-known British Methodist preacher William Sangster learned that he had progressive muscular atrophy and could not get well, he made four resolutions and kept them to the end: (1) I will never complain; (2) I will keep the home bright; (3) I will count my blessings; (4) I will try to turn it to gain. This is the approach to life that Solomon wants us to take.

However, we must note that Solomon is not saying, "Don't worry—be happy!" He is promoting faith in God, not "faith in faith" or "pie in the sky, by and by." Faith is only as good as the *object* of faith, and the greatest object of faith is the Lord. He can be trusted.

How can life be meaningless and monotonous for you when God has made you a part of His eternal plan? You are not an insignificant insect, crawling from one sad annihilation to another. If you have trusted Jesus Christ, you are a child of God being prepared for an eternal home. The Puritan pastor Thomas Watson said, "Eternity to the godly is a day that has no sunset; eternity to the wicked is a night that has no sunrise."

The proper attitude for us is fear of the Lord (v. 14),

> *"I know that there is nothing better for men than to be happy and do good while they live. That everyone may eat and drink, and find satisfaction in all his toil — this is the gift of God"*
> *(Ecclesiastes 3:12-13).*

....

which is not the cringing of a slave before a cruel master, but the submission of an obedient child to a loving parent. If we fear God, we need not fear anything else for He is in control.

Applying God's Truth:

1. What are four resolutions *you* could make to help you better cope with the difficult periods of life?

2. In what ways do you feel God is preparing you now for your eternal home?

3. How would you define "fear of the Lord" to someone hearing the phrase for the first time?

Read Ecclesiastes 4:1-6

Disorder in the Court

....

Solomon went into a courtroom to watch a trial, and there he saw innocent people being oppressed by power-hungry officials. The victims wept, but their tears did no good. Nobody stood with them to comfort or assist them. The oppressors had all the power and the victims were helpless to protest or ask for redress.

Why didn't Solomon do something about this injustice? After all, he was the king. Alas, even the king couldn't do a great deal to solve the problem. For once Solomon started to interfere with his government and reorganize things, he would only create new problems and reveal more corruption. This is not to suggest that we today should despair of cleaning out political corruption. As Christian citizens, we must pray for all in authority and do what we can to see that just laws are passed and fairly enforced. But it's doubtful that a huge administrative body like the one in Israel would ever be free of corruption, or that a "crusader" could have improved the situation.

Edward Gibbon, celebrated author of *The Decline and Fall of the Roman Empire,* said that political corruption was "the most infallible symptom of

> *"I saw the tears of the oppressed — and they have no comforter; power was on the side of their oppressors — and they have no comforter. And I declared that the dead, who had already died, are happier than the living, who are still alive"*
>
> *(Ecclesiastes 3:1-2).*

....

constitutional liberty." Perhaps he was right; for where there is freedom to obey, there is also freedom to disobey. Some of Solomon's officials decided they were above the law, and the innocent suffered.

Applying God's Truth:

1. In what ways do you think our court system permits injustices?

2. How do you feel when you become the victim of an injustice by someone wealthier or more influential than you? What, if anything, do you try to do to "right the scales of justice"?

3. Do you regularly pray for people in authority — even if they misuse their authority to take advantage of you and others?

Read **Ecclesiastes 4:7-16**

Two Threads Are Better Than One

....

Two are certainly better than one when it comes to *working* (v. 9) because two workers can get more done. Even when they divide the profits, they still get a better return for their efforts than if they had worked alone. Also, it's much easier to do difficult jobs together because one can be an encouragement to the other.

Two are better when it comes to *walking* (v. 10). Roads and paths in Palestine were not paved or even leveled, and there were many hidden rocks in the fields. It was not uncommon for even the most experienced traveler to stumble and fall, perhaps break a bone, or even fall into a hidden pit (Ex. 21:33-34). How wonderful to have a friend who can help you up (or out).

Two are better than one when it comes to *warmth* (v. 11). Two travelers camping out, or even staying in the courtyard of a public inn, would feel the cold of the Palestinian night and need one another's warmth for comfort. The only way to be "warm alone" is to carry extra blankets and add to your load.

Finally, two are better than one when it comes to their *watchcare,* especially at night (v. 12). It was

> *"Two are better than one, because they*
> *have a good return for their work"*
> *(Ecclesiastes 4:9).*

....

dangerous for anyone to travel alone, day or night; most people traveled in groups for fellowship and for safety.

If two travelers are better than one, then three would fare even better. Solomon had more than numbers in mind; he was also thinking of the unity involved in three cords woven together — what a beautiful picture of friendship!

Applying God's Truth:

1. What have you done lately to help someone's work go a little easier?

2. What have you done lately to assist someone who has stumbled in his or her *spiritual* walk and could use some help?

3. What kind of help could you use at this point in your life? Who might be able to help if you alerted that person to your need?

Read **Ecclesiastes 5:1-7**

The Sacrifice of Fools

....

Solomon had visited the courtroom, the marketplace, the highway, and the palace. Now he paid a visit to the temple, that magnificent building whose construction he had supervised. He watched the worshipers come and go, praising God, praying, sacrificing, and making vows. He noted that many of them were not at all sincere in their worship, and they left the sacred precincts in worse spiritual condition than when they had entered. What was their sin? They were robbing God of the reverence and honor that He deserved. Their acts of worship were perfunctory, insincere, and hypocritical.

Even though God's glorious presence doesn't dwell in our church buildings as it did in the temple, believers today still need to heed this warning. *The worship of God is the highest ministry of the church and must come from devoted hearts and yielded wills.* For God's people to participate in public worship while harboring unconfessed sin, is to ask for God's rebuke and judgment.

The important thing is that the worshiper "go near to listen," that is, to obey the Word of God. Sacrifices

> *"Guard your steps when you go to the house of God. Go near to listen rather than to offer the sacrifice of fools, who do not know that they do wrong"*
> *(Ecclesiastes 5:1).*

....

are not substitutes for obedience. Offerings in the hands without obedient faith in the heart become "the sacrifice of fools," because *only a fool thinks he can deceive God.* The fool thinks he is doing good, but he or she is only doing evil. And God knows it.

Applying God's Truth:

1. What kinds of "sacrifices" do people offer today that may be a substitute for genuine obedience to God?

2. What other forms of insincere worship take place in the church today?

3. How can you ensure that your own worship remains pure and sincere?

Read **Ecclesiastes 5:8-20**

Matters of Wealth and Health

There is no escaping the fact that we need a certain amount of money in order to live in this world, but money *of itself* is not the magic "cure-all" for every problem. John Wesley, cofounder of the Methodist Church, told his people, "Make all you can, save all you can, give all you can." Wesley himself could have been a very wealthy man, but he chose to live simply and give generously.

The late Joe Louis, world heavyweight boxing champion, used to say, "I don't like money, actually, but it quiets my nerves." But Solomon said that possessing wealth is no guarantee that your nerves will be calm and your sleep sound. According to him, the common laborer sleeps better than the rich man. *The Living Bible* expresses verse 12 perfectly: "The man who works hard sleeps well whether he eats little or much, but the rich must worry and suffer insomnia."

More than one preacher has mentioned John D. Rockefeller in his sermons as an example of a man whose life was almost ruined by wealth. At the age of fifty-three, Rockefeller was the world's only billionaire, earning about a million dollars a week. But he was a

> *"Whoever loves money never has money enough; whoever loves wealth is never satisfied with his income"*
> *(Ecclesiastes 5:10).*

....

sick man who lived on crackers and milk and could not sleep because of worry. When he started giving his money away, his health changed radically, and he lived to celebrate his ninety-eighth birthday!

Yes, it's good to have the things that money can buy, provided you don't lose the things that money can't buy.

Applying God's Truth:

1. Do you think there is a direct correlation between having an abundance of money and an abundance of peace? Why?

2. What do you think of Wesley's command to "Make all you can, save all you can, give all you can"?

3. To what extent do you think that worrying about money is a source of other problems in your life? In what ways?

Read **Ecclesiastes 6:1-9**

Living versus Existing

....

Rich and poor alike labor to stay alive. We must either produce food or earn money to buy it. The rich man can let his money work for him, but the poor man has to use his muscles if he and his family are going to eat. But even after all this labor, the appetite of neither one is fully satisfied.

Why does a person eat? So that he can add years to his life. But what good is it for me to add years to my life *if I don't add life to my years?* I'm like the birds that I watch in the backyard. They spend all their waking hours either looking for food or escaping from enemies. (We have cats in our neighborhood.) These birds are not really *living;* they are only *existing.* Yet they are fulfilling the purposes for which the Creator made them — and they even sing about it!

Solomon is not suggesting that it's wrong either to work or to eat. Many people enjoy doing both. But if life consists *only* in working and eating, then we are being controlled by our appetites and that almost puts us on the same level as animals. As far as nature is concerned, self-preservation may be the first law of life, but we who are made in the image of God must live for something higher.

*"All man's efforts are for his mouth, yet his
appetite is never satisfied"*
(Ecclesiastes 6:7).

....

Applying God's Truth:

1. Is your work a fulfilling activity for you? How might
   it become more fulfilling?

2. How much enjoyment do you get out of eating? Do
   you make the most out of your meals?

3. What things can you do to keep from letting routine
   activities (like working and eating) "take control"
   and prevent you from enjoying what is truly
   important in life?

Read **Ecclesiastes 6:10**

It's Your Choice

....

Since "what's going to be is going to be," why bother to make decisions? Isn't it all predestined anyway? "Whatever exists has already been named, and what man is has been known" (v. 10a). To the Jewish mind, giving a name to something is the same as fixing its character and stating what the thing really is. During the time of creation, God named the things that He made; and nobody changed those designations. "Light" is "light" and not "darkness"; "day" is "day" and not "night."

Our name is "man" — Adam, "from the earth" (Gen. 2:1). Nobody can change that: we came from the earth and we will return to the earth (Gen. 3:19). "Man" by any other name would still be "man," made from the dust and eventually returning to the dust.

The fact that God has named everything does not mean that our world is a prison and we have no freedom to act. Certainly God can accomplish His divine purposes with or without our cooperation, but He invites us to work with Him. We cooperate with God as we accept the "names" He has given to things: sin is sin; obedience is obedience; truth is truth. If we alter

"Better what the eye sees than the roving of the appetite. . . . Whatever exists has already been named, and what man is has been known"
(Ecclesiastes 6:10a).

....

these names, we move into a world of illusion and lose touch with reality. This is where many people are living today.

We are free to decide and choose our world, *but we are not free to change the consequences.* If we choose a world of illusion, we start living on substitutes, and there can be no satisfaction in a world of substitutes.

Applying God's Truth:

1. Does the fact that you serve an omniscient God make you feel that your life has less spontaneity and choice than it should have? Why?

2. What are some changes you would like to make in your life?

3. How do you think you might begin to "cooperate with God" to bring about some of the changes you have listed?

Read **Ecclesiastes 6:10b-12**

Questioning God
....

Solomon seems to say, "It just doesn't pay to argue with God or to fight God. This is the way life is, so just accept it and let God have His way. You can't win, and even if you do think you win, you ultimately lose."

But this is a negative view of the will of God. It gives the impression that God's will is a difficult and painful thing that should be avoided at all cost. Jesus said that God's will was the food that nourished and satisfied Him (John 4:32-34). It was meat, not medicine. The will of God comes from the heart of God and is an expression of the love of God. (See Ps. 33:11.) What God wills for us is best for us because He knows far more about us than we do.

Why would anyone want to have his or her "own way" just for the privilege of exercising "freedom"? Insisting on having our own way isn't freedom at all; it's the worst kind of bondage. In fact, the most terrible judgment we could experience in this life would be to have God "give us up" and let us have our own way (Rom. 1:24, 26, 28).

God is free to act as He sees best. He is not a

> *"No man can contend with one who is*
> *stronger than he"*
> *(Ecclesiastes 6:10b).*

....

prisoner of His attributes, His creation, or His eternal
purposes. You and I may not understand how God
exercises His freedom, but it isn't necessary for us to
know all. Our greatest freedom comes when we are
lovingly lost in the will of God. Our Father in heaven
doesn't feel threatened when we question Him, debate
with Him, or even wrestle with Him, so long as we love
His will and want to please Him.

Applying God's Truth:

1. What kind of emotions does the thought of "God's
   will" bring to your heart?

2. Do you think God is displeased when you question
   His will for you? Why?

3. Is it easy for you to trust that God knows best and
   leave things in His hands? Or do you want to
   understand everything that's going on as it is
   happening?

Read **Ecclesiastes 7:1-8**

Looking Death in the Face

....

Solomon was not contrasting *birth* and *death,* nor was he suggesting that it is better to die than to be born because you can't die unless you have been born. He was contrasting two significant days in human experience: the day a person receives his or her name and the day when that name shows up in the obituary column. The life lived between those two events will determine whether that name leaves behind a lovely fragrance or a foul stench.

Solomon advised the people to look death in the face and learn from it. He did not say that we should be preoccupied with death because that could be abnormal. But there is a danger that we might try to avoid confrontations with the reality of death and, as a result, not take life as seriously as we should. "Teach us to number our days aright, that we may gain a heart of wisdom" (Ps. 90:12).

The late Dr. Ernest Becker wrote in his Pulitzer-Prize-winning book *The Denial of Death:* " . . . the idea of death, the fear of it, haunts the human animal like nothing else; it is a mainspring of human activity—activity designed largely to avoid the fatality

> *"A good name is better than fine perfume,*
> *and the day of death better than the day*
> *of birth"*
> *(Ecclesiastes 7:1).*

....

of death, to overcome it by denying in some way that it
is the final destiny for man" (Free Press, 1975, p. ix).
King Solomon knew this truth centuries ago!

Applying God's Truth:

1. In what ways does thinking about death help you
   take life more seriously?

2. Would you say you spend more time thinking back
   about the things you've done since you were born,
   or thinking about what you hope to do before you
   die? Are you satisfied that your balance of the two is
   what it should be?

3. Would you say you are haunted by the fear of death,
   or is your eventual death something that inspires
   you to a greater faith in God? Explain.

Read **Ecclesiastes 7:9-12**

Seize the Day
....

An Arab proverb says, "Watch your beginnings." Good beginnings will usually mean good endings. The Prodigal Son started with happiness and wealth, but ended with suffering and poverty (Luke 15:11-24). Joseph began as a slave but ended up a sovereign! God always saves "the best wine" until the last (John 2:10), but Satan starts with his "best" and then leads the sinner into suffering and perhaps even death.

When life is difficult and we are impatient for change, it is easy to long for "the good old days" when things were better. When the foundation was laid for the second temple, the old men wept for "the good old days" and the young men sang because the work had begun (Ezra 3:12-13). It has been said that "the good old days" are the combination of a bad memory and a good imagination, and often this is true.

Yesterday is past and cannot be changed, and tomorrow may not come; so make the most of today. *"Carpe diem!"* wrote the Roman poet Horace. "Seize the day!" This does not mean we shouldn't learn from the past or prepare for the future because both are important. It means that we must live *today* in the will

> *"Do not say, 'Why were the old days better than these?' For it is not wise to ask such questions"*
> *(Ecclesiastes 7:10).*

....

of God and not be paralyzed by yesterday or hypnotized by tomorrow. The Victorian essayist Hilaire Belloc wrote, "While you are dreaming of the future or regretting the past, the present, which is all you have, slips from you and is gone."

Applying God's Truth:

1. In what ways do you try to "watch your beginnings"? Do you keep God's will in mind as you make plans?

2. When times are difficult, what are some things you can do to maintain a focus on the future rather than drifting into a longing for the past?

3. What can you do right now to "seize" *today?*

Read *Ecclesiastes 7:13-29*

The Best of Times, The Worst of Times

....

Wisdom gives us perspective so that we aren't discouraged when times are difficult or arrogant when things are going well. It takes a good deal of spirituality to be able to accept prosperity as well as adversity, for often prosperity does greater damage.

God balances our lives by giving us enough blessings to keep us happy and enough burdens to keep us humble. If all we had were blessings in our hands, we would fall right over, so the Lord balances the blessings in our hands with burdens on our backs. That helps to keep us steady, and as we yield to Him, He can even turn the burdens into blessings.

Why does God constitute our lives in this way? The answer is simple: to keep us from thinking we know it all and that we can manage our lives by ourselves. "A man cannot discover anything about his future" (v. 14). Just about the time we think we have an explanation for things, God changes the situation and we have to throw out our formula. This is where Job's friends went wrong: they tried to use an old road map to guide Job on a brand-new journey, and the map didn't fit. No matter how much experience we have in

> *"When times are good, be happy; but when times are bad, consider: God has made the one as well as the other. Therefore, a man cannot discover anything about his future"*
> *(Ecclesiastes 7:14).*

....

the Christian life, or how many books we read, we must still walk by faith.

Applying God's Truth:

1. Can you think of a recent time when you became discouraged during difficult times? Or when you were arrogant when things were going well?

2. Do you feel you have a level of wisdom adequate enough to allow you to accept both adversity and prosperity? If not, what do you think you need to do?

3. During times of adversity do you try to see what God might be trying to teach you? Or are you usually too busy complaining?

Read *Ecclesiastes 8:1-13*

It Just Isn't Fair

....

If there is no God, then we have nobody to blame but ourselves (or fate) for what happens in the world. But if we believe in a good and loving God, we must face the difficult question of why there is so much suffering in the world. Does God know about it and yet not care? Or does He know and care but lack the power to do anything about it?

Some people ponder this question and end up becoming either agnostics or atheists, but in so doing, they create a whole new problem: "Where does all the *good* come from in the world?" It's difficult to believe that matter *alone* produced the beautiful and enjoyable things we have in our world, even in the midst of so much evil.

Other people solve the problem by saying that evil is only an illusion and we shouldn't worry about it, or that God is in the process of "evolving" and can't do much about the tragedies of life. They assure us that God will get stronger and things will improve as the process of evolution goes on.

Solomon didn't deny the existence of God or the

*"Although a wicked man commits a
hundred crimes and still lives a long time, I
know that it will go better with God-fearing
men, who are reverent before God"*
(Ecclesiastes 8:12).

....

reality of evil, nor did he limit the power of God.
Solomon solved the problem of evil by affirming these
factors *and seeing them in their proper perspective.*

During the darkest days of World War II, somebody
asked a friend of mine, "Why doesn't God stop the
war?" My friend wisely replied, "Because He didn't
start it in the first place." Solomon would have agreed
with that answer.

Applying God's Truth:

1. When people ask your opinion, how do you explain
   the existence of suffering?

2. Do you think God's power or His love are limited in
   any way? Explain.

3. Are you suffering in some way in which you need to
   apply what you believe?

Read **Ecclesiastes 8:14-17**

The First Step toward Knowledge

....

The person who has to know everything, or who thinks he knows everything, is destined for disappointment in this world. Through many difficult days and sleepless nights, the Preacher applied himself diligently to the mysteries of life. He came to the conclusion that "no one can comprehend what goes on under the sun" (v. 17). Perhaps we can solve a puzzle here and there, but no man or woman can comprehend the totality of things or explain all that God is doing.

Historian Will Durant surveyed human history in his multivolume *Story of Civilization* and came to the conclusion that "our knowledge is a receding mirage in an expanding desert of ignorance." Of course, this fact must not be used as an excuse for stupidity. "The secret things belong to the LORD our God, but the things revealed belong to us and to our children forever, that we may follow all the words of this law" (Deut. 29:29). God doesn't expect us to know the unknowable, but He does expect us to learn all that we can and obey what He teaches us. In fact, the more we obey, the more He will teach us (John 7:17).

A confession of ignorance is the first step toward

> *"No one can comprehend what goes on under the sun. Despite all his efforts to search it out, man cannot discover its meaning"*
> *(Ecclesiastes 8:17).*

....

true knowledge. "The man who thinks he knows something does not yet know as he ought to know" (1 Cor. 8:2). The person who wants to learn God's truth must possess honesty and humility.

Applying God's Truth:

1. What are some of the mysteries of life that you frequently ponder?

2. How is your faith affected when you struggle with something you can't figure out?

3. Do you think there are things God doesn't want us to know, or should we keep struggling to understand the mysteries of life?

Read **Ecclesiastes 9:1-4**

A Final Appointment

....

"I'm not afraid to die," quipped Woody Allen, "I just don't want to be there when it happens." But he *will* be there when it happens, as must every human being, because there is no escaping death when your time has come. Death is not an accident, it's an appointment (Heb. 9:27), a destiny that nobody but God can cancel or change.

Life and death are "in the hand of God" (Ecc. 9:1), and only He knows our future, whether it will bring blessing ("love") or sorrow ("hatred"). Solomon was not suggesting that we are passive actors in a cosmic drama, following an unchangeable script handed to us by an uncaring director. Throughout this book, Solomon has emphasized our freedom of discernment and decision. But only God knows what the future holds for us and what will happen tomorrow because of the decisions we make today.

"As it is with the good man, so with the sinner" (v. 2). "If so, why bother to live a godly life?" someone may ask. "After all, whether we obey the Law or disobey, bring sacrifices or neglect them, make or break promises, we will die just the same." Yes, we share a

> *"Anyone who is among the living has hope—even a live dog is better off than a dead lion!"*
>
> *(Ecclesiastes 9:4)*

....

common destiny on earth—death and the grave—*but we do not share a common destiny in eternity.* For that reason, everybody must honestly face "the last enemy" (1 Cor. 15:26) and decide how to deal with it. How people deal with the reality of death reveals itself in the way they deal with the realities of life.

Applying God's Truth:

1. Have you placed your life "in the hand of God"? How about your death?

2. Is there anything you feel you need to do before you die? If so, are you working toward getting it done?

3. Does thinking about death inspire you to greater action, or frighten you into passivity?

*Read **Ecclesiastes 9:5-10***

When Hope Becomes Hopeless

....

What Solomon wrote about the dead can be "reversed" and applied to the living. The dead do not know what is happening on earth, but the living know and can respond to it. The dead cannot add anything to their reward or their reputation, but the living can. The dead cannot relate to people on earth by loving, hating, or envying, but the living can. Solomon was emphasizing the importance of seizing opportunities while we live, rather than blindly hoping for something better in the future, because death will end our opportunities on this earth.

"The human body experiences a powerful gravitational pull in the direction of hope," wrote journalist Norman Cousins, who himself survived a near-fatal illness and a massive heart attack. "That is why the patient's hopes are the physician's secret weapon. They are the hidden ingredients in any prescription."

We endure because we hope, but "hope in hope" (like "faith in faith") is too often only a kind of self-hypnosis that keeps us from facing life honestly. While a patient may be better off with an optimistic attitude,

> *"The living know that they will die, but the dead know nothing; they have no further reward, and even the memory of them is forgotten"*
> *(Ecclesiastes 9:5).*

....

it is dangerous for him to follow a *false hope* that may keep him from preparing for death. That kind of hope is hopeless. When the end comes, the patient's *outlook* may be cheerful, but the *outcome* will be tragic.

Applying God's Truth:

1. If you knew you were to die soon, would your plans for today change in any way? How?

2. What are some opportunities you need to seize while you still have the opportunity?

3. What is your definition of *hope*? Does your hope keep your faith strong?

Read **Ecclesiastes 9:11-18**

No Guarantees

·····································

Anticipating the response of his listeners (and his readers), Solomon turned from his discussion of death and began to discuss life. "If death is unavoidable," somebody would argue, "then the smartest thing we can do is major on our strengths and concentrate on life. When death comes, at least we'll have the satisfaction of knowing we worked hard and achieved some success."

"Don't be too sure of that!" was Solomon's reply. "You can't guarantee what will happen in life, because life is unpredictable."

Our abilities are no guarantee of success (vv. 11-12). While it is generally true that the fastest runners win the races, the strongest soldiers win the battles, and the smartest and most skillful workers win the best jobs, it is also true that these same gifted people can fail miserably because of factors out of their control. The successful person knows how to make the most of "time and procedure" (8:5), but only the Lord can control "time and chance" (v. 11).

Of course, Christians don't depend on such things

> *"The race is not to the swift or the battle to the strong, nor does food come to the wise or wealth to the brilliant or favor to the learned; but time and chance happen to them all"*
> *(Ecclesiastes 9:11).*

....

as "luck" or "chance" because their confidence is in the loving providence of God. A dedicated Christian doesn't carry a rabbit's foot or trust in lucky days or numbers. Canadian humorist Stephen Leacock said, "I'm a great believer in luck. I find that the harder I work, the more I have of it." Christians trust God to guide them and help them in making decisions, and they believe that His will is best. They leave "time and chance" in His capable hands.

Applying God's Truth:

1. What would you say are your most significant strengths? In what ways do you try to count on those strengths for success?

2. Do you have any personal superstitions? To what extent do you tend to rely on luck or chance?

3. From this point on, how can you better leave "time and chance" completely in God's hands?

Read **Ecclesiastes 10:1-10**

Foolish Rulers

....

If there is one person who needs wisdom, it is the ruler of a nation. When God asked Solomon what gift he especially wanted, the king asked for wisdom (1 Kings 3:3-28). Lyndon B. Johnson said, "A president's hardest task is not to *do* what's right, but to *know* what's right." That requires wisdom.

If a ruler is *proud,* he may say and do foolish things that cause him to lose the respect of his associates (v. 4). The picture here is of a proud ruler who easily becomes angry and takes out his anger on the attendants around him. Of course, if a man has no control over himself, how can he hope to have control over his people?

To be sure, there is a righteous anger that sometimes needs to be displayed (Eph. 4:26), but not everything we call "righteous indignation" is really "righteous." It is so easy to give vent to jealousy and malice by disguising them as holy zeal for God. Not every religious crusader is motivated by love for God or obedience to the Word. His or her zeal could be a mask that is covering hidden anger or jealousy.

But if a ruler is too *pliable,* he is also a fool (vv. 5-7).

> *"Fools are put in many high positions, while the rich occupy the low ones. I have seen slaves on horseback, while princes go on foot like slaves"*
> *(Ecclesiastes 10:6-7).*

....

If he lacks character and courage, he will put fools in the high offices and qualified people in the low offices. The servants will ride on horses while the noblemen will walk. If a ruler has incompetent people advising him, he is almost certain to govern the nation unwisely.

The best rulers (and leaders) are men and women who are tough-minded but tenderhearted, who put the best people on the horses and don't apologize for it.

Applying God's Truth:

1. What bosses have you most respected? Which have you least respected? What caused the differences in your opinions?

2. Do you feel that you have sufficient control over yourself so that you can help control others? If not, what areas do you need to work on?

3. Would you say you are too proud? Too pliable? Or do you feel you are achieving an appropriate balance?

*Read **Ecclesiastes 10:11-20***

Looking Out for Number One

....

In recent years, various developing nations have seen how easy it is for unscrupulous leaders to steal government funds in order to build their own kingdoms. Unfortunately, it has also happened recently to some religious organizations. The courts might not catch up with all the unscrupulous politicians, but God will eventually judge them, and His judgment will be just.

The familiar saying "A little bird told me" probably originated from verse 20. You can imagine a group of these officers having a party in one of their private rooms and, instead of toasting the king, they are cursing ["making light of"] him. Of course, they wouldn't do this if any of the king's friends were present, but they were sure that the company would faithfully keep the secret. Alas, somebody told the king what was said, and this gave him reason to punish them or dismiss them from their offices.

Even if we can't respect the person in the office, we must respect the office (Rom. 13:1-7; 1 Peter 2:13-17). "You shall not revile God, nor curse a ruler of your people" (Ex. 22:28). These hirelings were certainly

> *"Do not revile the king even in your thoughts, or curse the rich in your bedroom, because a bird of the air may carry your words, and a bird on the wing may report what you say"*
> (Ecclesiastes 10:20).

....

indiscreet when they cursed the king, for they should have known that one of their number would use this event either to intimidate his friends or to ingratiate himself with the ruler. A statesman asks, "What is best for my country?" A politician asks, "What is best for my party?" But a mere officeholder, a hireling, asks, "What is safest and most profitable for me?"

Applying God's Truth:

1. Do you know of any ministries or religious organizations that have been shaken by scandals concerning their leaders? What was the root of the problem? What were the results?

2. Can you think of anything you've said today that might embarrass you if "a little bird" passed it along to someone else?

3. Think of some leaders you don't particularly respect. What can you do to at least respect the office, if not the person?

Read **Ecclesiastes 11**

A Quest for Adventure

....

When I was a boy, I practically lived in the public library during the summer months. I loved books, the building was cool, and the librarians gave me the run of the place since I was one of their best customers. One summer I read nothing but true adventure stories written by real heroes like Frank Buck and Martin Johnson. These men knew the African jungles better than I knew my hometown! I was fascinated by *I Married Adventure,* the autobiography of Martin Johnson's wife Osa. When Clyde Beatty brought his circus to town, I was in the front row watching him "tame" the lions.

Since those boyhood days, life has become a lot calmer for me, but I trust I haven't lost that sense of adventure. In fact, as I get older, I'm asking God to keep me from getting set in my ways in a life that is routine, boring, and predictable. "I don't want my life to end in a swamp," said British expositor F.B. Meyer. I agree with him. When I trusted Jesus Christ as my Savior, "I married adventure"; and that meant living by faith and expecting the unexpected.

Solomon used two activities to illustrate his point:

*"Cast your bread upon the waters, for after
many days you will find it again"*
(Ecclesiastes 11:1).

....

the merchant sending out his ships (vv. 1-2) and the
farmer sowing his seed (vv. 3-6). In both activities, a
great deal of faith is required because neither the
merchant nor the farmer can control the
circumstances. If the merchant and the farmer waited
until the circumstances were ideal, they would never
get anything done! Life has a certain amount of risk to
it, and that's where faith comes in.

Applying God's Truth:

1. What was the last adventurous thing you did?

2. If you had a bit more faith in God, what new
   adventure might you like to try?

3. What is your usual attitude toward risk? Are you
   satisfied with it, or would you like to become more
   (or less) a risk-taker? How might you make any
   desired changes?

DAY **30**

*Read **Ecclesiastes 12***

Satisfaction Guaranteed

....

People may seem to get away with sin (8:11), but their sins will eventually be exposed and judged righteously. Those who have not trusted the Lord Jesus Christ will be doomed forever. "The eternity of punishment is a thought which crushes the heart," said Charles Spurgeon. "The Lord God is slow to anger, but when He is once aroused to it, as He will be against those who finally reject His Son, He will put forth all His omnipotence to crush His enemies."

Six times in his discourse, Solomon told us to enjoy life while we can; but at no time did he advise us to enjoy sin. The joys of the present depend on the security of the future. If you know Jesus Christ as your Savior, then your sins have already been judged on the cross; and "there is now no condemnation for those who are in Christ Jesus" (Rom. 8:1 and see John 5:24). But if you die having never trusted Christ, you will face judgment at His throne and be lost forever (Rev. 20:11-15).

Is life worth living? Yes, *if you are truly alive through faith in Jesus Christ.* Then you can be satisfied, no matter what God may permit to come to your life.

*"Fear God and keep His commandments,
for this is the whole duty of man. For God
will bring every deed into judgment,
including every hidden thing, whether it
is good or evil"*
(Ecclesiastes 12:13-14).

....

"He who has the Son has life; he who does not have
the Son of God does not have life" (1 John 5:12).

You can receive life in Christ and — *be satisfied!*

Applying God's Truth:

1. Do you know of someone who truly seems to think
   he or she will "get by" with his or her sinful actions?
   What can you learn from this person?

2. Do you feel more satisfied with life now than you did
   when you began these readings? In what ways?
   What areas of life do you still need to work on?

3. What are three things you can do from now on that
   are likely to bring you a greater degree of
   satisfaction with life?